North Devon's Lost Railways

by

Peter Dale

A Bulleid Light Pacific leaving Barnstaple Junction with an Ilfracombe train.
This was Barnstaple's first station and is still open, renamed simply as Barnstaple.

ACKNOWLEDGMENTS
I would like to thank my father who first fired my interest in railways and Ken Jones who introduced me to this project.
The publishers wish to thank the following for permission to reproduce the photographs in this book: John Alsop for pages 1, 2, 4, 5–12 (both), 13–15 (both), 16–25, 27, 28, 30, 32–41 (both), 42–46, the inside back cover and the back cover; the Rev. D.J. Lane for pages 1, 3 and 29; W.A.C. Smith for pages 31, 47 and 48; and Neville Stead for the inside front cover (photograph by D.P. Leckonby) and page 26.

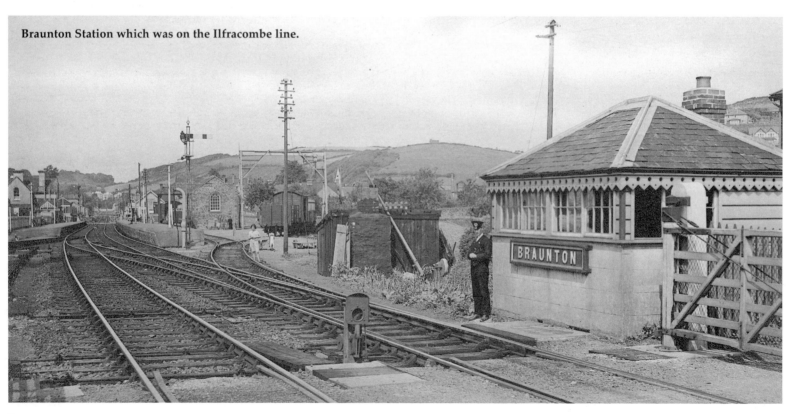

Braunton Station which was on the Ilfracombe line.

INTRODUCTION

North Devon was dominated by the London & South Western Railway (LSWR), with the Great Western Railway (GWR) being of lesser importance. The early lines built to connect with the Bristol & Exeter Railway (such as the North Devon line from Crediton to Barnstaple) were built to the Great Western's 7 feet broad gauge and north Devon was an important battleground between the use of this and standard gauge of 4 feet 8½ inches used by the LSWR. The line from Crediton to Barnstaple finally became part of the LSWR (it even owned some broad gauge locomotives for a time), but there were many tussles and broken agreements over the spread of railways into north Devon. In 1876 the Bristol & Exeter was amalgamated with the GWR which eventually lost the 'Battle of the Gauges' and the last 7 feet gauge express ran in May 1892.

Development of the area for holidays came in the twentieth century with llfracombe and Lynton and Lynmouth being the major coastal resorts. The new century also brought the first road competition and both the GWR and the LSWR developed bus services. These were later sold off, although it is worth mentioning that the Lynton & Barnstaple Railway was the first railway to provide a bus service in May 1903. It ran from Blackmoor (on the L&BR) to llfracombe but was soon withdrawn after objections from the police to speeds in excess of 8 m.p.h. and the buses were sold to the GWR to inaugurate its first bus service to The Lizard.

In 1923 the old railway companies were grouped into four. In Devon the LSWR became part of the Southern Railway, while the GWR continued in an enlarged form. Despite increasing competition from road travel, most lines continued through nationalisation in 1948 until the Beeching era.

The lines have been arranged in this book in the order of a leisurely journey from Exeter to Plymouth, using timetables of the 1920s. The journey worked out includes a trip on the

Bideford, Westward Ho! & Appledore Railway (purists may object that this is impossible as it closed before the North Devon & Cornwall Junction opened, but this is an exercise in nostalgia). Leaving Exeter in mid-morning we travel by the Exe Valley to Tiverton and then to Tiverton Junction. Here we cross the mainline and catch the Culm Valley train to Hemyock where we arrive in time for lunch. We retrace our steps to get back to Tiverton in the late afternoon and continue our journey on the Exe Valley and change at Dulverton to arrive in the evening at Barnstaple (Victoria Road). The next day we go to Barnstaple Town and catch the train to Lynton, returning to Barnstaple just after noon. After lunch we catch the train to llfracombe (from the Town station) and return to Barnstaple Junction later on. From here it is only a 20 minute journey to Bideford, where we walk across the bridge to the town and Bideford Quay from where we take a return trip on the Bideford, Westward Ho! & Appledore line. On the following day we travel to Halwill Junction and get a return ticket to Bude. We are back at Halwill Junction in time for a train to Launceston. From here we could return to Okehampton and thence to Plymouth or we could catch a GWR train to Plymouth, in either case to arrive in the middle of the evening.

It is hoped that these pictures revive pleasant memories of holidays by the sea for some and may encourage others to see what is left of our railway heritage.

The autotrain for Tiverton Junction (the 'Tivvy Bumper') at Tiverton Station.

Exe Valley line

			Stations closed	Date
Passenger service withdrawn	7 October 1963		Burn Halt	7 October 1963
Distance	19.4 miles		Cadeleigh **	7 October 1963
Company	Great Western Railway		West Exe Halt	7 October 1963
			Tiverton	5 October 1964
Stations closed	*Date*		Bolham Halt	7 October 1963
Brampford Speke	7 October 1963		Cove Halt	7 October 1963
Thorverton	7 October 1963		Bampton ***	7 October 1963
Up Exe Halt *	7 October 1963			

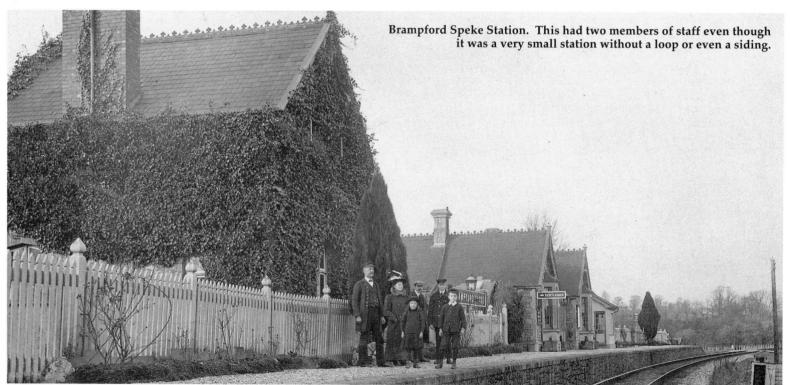

Brampford Speke Station. This had two members of staff even though it was a very small station without a loop or even a siding.

* Known as Up Exe and Silverton until 1 May 1905 and then as Up Exe until 1 October 1923.
** Known as Cadeleigh and Bickleigh until May 1906.

*** From 1911 the station appeared in timetables as Bampton (Devon) to avoid confusion with a station of the same name in Oxfordshire.

Although the station building at Thorverton was similar to that of Brampford Speke, this station had a passing loop, a goods yard and shed, and a siding to a grain mill.

This line, between Morebath Junction (on the GWR route to Barnstaple) and Stoke Canon (on the GWR West of England mainline), opened in two parts. The first of these was the Tiverton & North Devon Railway which opened in August 1884 and was worked by the GWR, while the southern section, the Exe Valley Railway, opened in May 1885, having already been taken over by the GWR. Both lines were standard gauge. Very much a rural railway, the line was the haunt of autotrains but was very useful when the lower Culm Valley flooded. At these times the mainline between Stoke Canon and Cullompton can be impassable, a problem exacerbated when ballast is washed away. Up trains were diverted via Tiverton to Tiverton Junction where they rejoined the mainline, but because of the junction arrangements at Tiverton Junction down trains were worked via Dulverton and the Devon and Somerset Railway. The line had a yellow route classification which meant that the heavier classes of locomotives were not allowed over it, but in practice blue classification locomotives such as 'Big Prairies' (e.g. 41XX) and 43XX Moguls were allowed to work diverted trains (blue class locomotives were heavier than yellow, but a blind eye was turned). Now when the mainline is flooded services are simply suspended. The last day of service was a sad event, made even more so by the unexpected provision of diesel traction in the shape of class 22 diesel hydraulics.

Cadeleigh Station, photographed before 1906 when it was still known as Cadeleigh and Bickleigh. At the end of the train in the centre note the vehicle transporting gas which was possibly used for station lighting somewhere along the line.

Bickleigh Station

On the Exe Valley line near Bampton.

EXE VALLEY RAILWAY Nr BAMPTON 8386

Bampton Station. Besides the loop and goods yard here, there was also a line to a stone quarry which carried a lot of traffic.

Tiverton branch

Passenger service withdrawn	5 October 1964	*Stations closed*	*Date*
Distance	4.8 miles	Tiverton *	5 October 1964
Company	Bristol & Exeter Railway	Halberton Halt	5 October 1964

Tiverton Station. The Tiverton Junction train is on the right while the train entering the station is bound for Dulverton.

Opened in June 1848, this line was built as a broad gauge branch of the B&ER and was specifically designed to reach Tiverton which had been bypassed by the mainline despite its importance as the third largest town in Devon (according to the 1831 census). Construction of the line faced strong opposition from the Grand Western Canal Company which did not want to lose traffic, and this was only overcome when the B&ER leased the canal and finally purchased it outright in 1863. Trains were generally timed to connect with mainline trains at the junction. A shuttle service was run and after the introduction of autotrains in 1927 the service was nicknamed the 'Tivvy Bumper' and unusually it ran without a guard, the driver being responsible for the train. The locomotive on the last train, no. 1450, has been preserved in working order and is used on various preserved railways; another member of the class resides in Tiverton Museum.

* This replaced the original B&ER station of the same name in 1885.

Culm Valley Light Railway

Passenger service withdrawn	7 September 1963	*Stations closed*	*Date*
Distance	7.3 miles	Coldharbour Halt	7 September 1963
Company	Culm Valley Light Railway	Uffculme	7 September 1963
		Culmstock	7 September 1963
		Whitehall Halt	7 September 1963
		Hemyock	7 September 1963

Uffculme Station. The presence of a saddle tank locomotive probably dates the picture to the mid-1890s.

Culmstock Station. There was a loop into the goods shed here. The train is a 14XX 0-4-2T with an ex-Barry Railway coach.

The Culm Valley Light Railway opened between Tiverton Junction on the GWR Exeter to Taunton mainline and Hemyock in May 1876. It was worked by the GWR from the outset. The engineer of the line was Arthur Pain, an early supporter of light railways who was later engineer to the 3 feet gauge Southwold Railway. The line was built using 40lb rails and the B&ER built locomotives for it that had an especially light axle load. There was a maximum speed of only 15 m.p.h. and some mixed trains could take an hour for the journey of just over 7 miles. Even in its later years the line still did not resemble a typical GWR branch, despite being worked by 14XX class tanks. Because of the line's light construction it often used rolling stock passed down from other lines instead of standard GWR rolling stock, and it ended its days with two ex-Barry Railway coaches that had been rebuilt with gas lighting as speeds on the line were too low for dynamos to charge batteries. The line was known for its dairy traffic from Hemyock, but that was eventually lost to road competition.

Two views of Hemyock Station: the one on the left shows it as the epitome of the country station while the other shows how appearances can be deceptive as the station was actually dominated by the local dairy. Unsightly though it is, it provided much of the line's raison d'etre.

Devon & Somerset Railway *

Passenger service withdrawn	3 October 1966	*Stations closed*	*Date*
Distance	42.6 miles	Dulverton	3 October 1966
	(North Fitzwarren to Barnstaple)	East Anstey	3 October 1966
Company	Devon & Somerset Railway	Yeo Mill Halt	3 October 1966
		Bishop's Nympton and Molland ***	3 October 1966
Stations closed	*Date*	South Molton	3 October 1966
Venn Cross **	3 October 1966	Filleigh ****	3 October 1966
Morebath	3 October 1966	Swimbridge	3 October 1966
Morebath Junction Halt	3 October 1966	Barnstaple (Victoria Road) *****	13 June 1960

Morebath Station. The village was about 1 ½ miles away.

* Closed stations on this line that were in Somerset were Milverton, Wiveliscombe and Dulverton.

** This station straddled the county border with Somerset.

*** Known as Molland until 1 March 1876.

**** Known as Castle Hill until 1 January 1881.

***** After this date trains were diverted to Barnstaple Junction.

East Anstey Station, August 1966.

This broad gauge line was opened to Barnstaple in November 1873 and was leased by the B&ER. There were many financial difficulties and when supplies ran out during construction a party of seventy navvies, armed with clubs, marched on Wiveliscombe to demand bread and beer. The initial train service was very poor but improved later as it was the GWR's route not only to Barnstaple, but also to the resort of Ilfracombe. Ultimately, the Cornish Riviera Express carried a slip coach for Ilfracombe that was slipped at Taunton and worked over the line, while the 9.00 a.m. from Paddington carried a restaurant car that worked to Barnstaple. The GWR route to Barnstaple from Paddington via Taunton was considerably shorter than the Southern route from Waterloo via Exeter – in 1939 the journey time from Paddington to Barnstaple was 4 hours and 35 minutes, compared to 5 hours exactly by the Southern's crack Atlantic Coast Express. Despite this, trains were diverted to the Southern route in the 1960s and even trains travelling via Taunton to Ilfracombe were made to go through Exeter. At one time there was a daily 'rabbit special' (which conveyed the beasts to butchers' markets) from South Molton, but myxomatosis put paid to that.

Right: Bishop's Nympton & Molland Station. Molland was about 2 miles north east of the station and Bishop's Nympton 3 miles south west.

South Molton Station. There was not much difference in the appearance of these stations, both photographed in August 1966.

An inspection train on what is likely to be Castle Hill Viaduct which was on the line near Filleigh.

Filleigh Station, August 1966. In earlier days there was a private siding here but the passing loop had been lifted by the time this picture was taken.

Swimbridge Station, August 1966. The second platform was added in February 1904. Only the car on the right indicates the march of progress.

Lynton & Barnstaple Railway

Passenger service withdrawn	29 September 1935	*Stations closed*	*Date*
Distance	19.3 miles	Bratton Fleming	29 September 1935
Company	Lynton & Barnstaple Railway	Blackmoor	29 September 1935
		Parracombe Halt	29 September 1935
Stations closed	*Date*	Woody Bay	29 September 1935
Snapper Halt	29 September 1935	Caffyns Halt	29 September 1935
Chelfham	29 September 1935	Lynton	29 September 1935

A Manning Wardle, 'Yeo', with a mixed train at Snapper Halt. It looks as though the cart, on the flat wagon, is at the limit of the loading gauge.

Chelfham Station. The viaduct here, which still stands, is behind the photographer.

This 1 foot 11½ inch gauge line opened in May 1898 and was the culmination of a number of attempts to link the resorts of Lynton and Lynmouth with the rest of the country. The route crossed Exmoor from a junction with the LSWR at Barnstaple Town Station (on the line to Ilfracombe) to its terminus at Lynton, 700 feet above sea level. The line was worked by some Manning Wardle 2-6-2Ts and one Baldwin 2-4-2T and remained independent until 1923 when it became part of the Southern Railway. After 1923 the Southern invested in the line, a new locomotive was provided, and the older ones were shipped off to Eastleigh to be overhauled. Lynton Station was enlarged and the coaching stock was also improved. Summer weekends could be quite busy with excursions connecting with trains from many places on the Southern system.

Bratton Fleming Station.

In the 1930s economies began to be made, while footwarmers (a primitive form of heating in which hot water was put into a metal tank on the floor of the carriage – a luxury usually only given to first class passengers) on the services were replaced by steam heating to try to encourage winter passengers. Eventually, improvements to local roads and competing bus services meant that few local people used the line. A meeting, held in Barnstaple, to discuss the line's future was attended by people from Lynton who travelled in by car. Closure came at the end of the 1935 summer season. The line was a favourite with enthusiasts but its closure preceded the preservation era by about fifteen years. Despite that a group of enthusiasts are currently working to re-open part of the line.

Blackmoor Station, photographed in October 1947, by which time it had been extended and converted into a hotel.

Two 2-6-2T locomotives, nos. 188 (the pilot) and 759, taking water at Parracombe. This was the last train: 29 September 1935.

Woody Bay Station. Down trains used to stop here for the collection of tickets from passengers.

Lynton.   Railway Station.

The American (Baldwin) 2-4-2T, 'Lyn',
waiting at the loop at Lynton Station.

Ilfracombe line

Passenger service withdrawn	5 October 1970	*Stations closed*	*Date*
Distance	14.9 miles	Barnstaple Town	5 October 1970
Company	London & South Western Railway	Wrafton	5 October 1970
		Braunton	5 October 1970
		Morthoe	5 October 1970
		Ilfracombe	5 October 1970

**A West Country class, no. 34003, 'Plymouth', leaving Barnstaple Town
for Barnstaple Junction and crossing the viaduct over the River Taw.**

Wrafton Station, September 1967.

This line was built by the Barnstaple & Ilfracombe Railway, a subsidiary of the LSWR, and opened on 20 July 1874. The line was later doubled, excepting the bridge over the River Taw at Barnstaple, and carried heavy holiday traffic from both the GWR and LSWR routes to Barnstaple. Much of the traffic in later years was routed via the Southern route through Exeter, 22 miles further than via Taunton on the GWR route. This discouraged traffic and by the 1960s most passengers arrived in Ilfracombe by road. In 1947 Ilfracombe became the western terminus of the Devon Belle, a new Pullman service from Waterloo. This was quite popular and two trains were needed, accompanied by a stylish observation car which had to be turned on the turntable just like a locomotive. One of these cars has been preserved and runs on the Paignton & Dartmouth Railway.

Braunton Station.

A Bulleid at Morthoe Station. Note the signal post built from rails,
a common economy measure used by the Southern Railway.

243.

A pre-grouping view of Ilfracombe Station.

ILFRACOMBE

A Class N 2-6-0, no. 31841, at Ilfracombe with the 7.00 p.m. service to Barnstaple Junction, August 1960.

Barnstaple – Torrington

Passenger service withdrawn	4 October 1965	*Stations closed*	*Date*
Distance	14.3 miles	Fremington	4 October 1965
Company	North Devon Railway/	Instow	4 October 1965
	Bideford Extension Railway	Bideford	4 October 1965
		Torrington	4 October 1965

There was considerable freight traffic, both incoming and outgoing, at Fremington Station.

Fremington Station, September 1967.

After much argument, this line opened as a broad gauge from Barnstaple Junction to Bideford on 2 November 1855, and to Torrington on 18 July 1872 (Barnstaple to Fremington was originally narrow gauge but was widened). In its earliest days, Thomas Brassey, the line's contractor, ran trains using his own locomotives and rolling stock to Crediton, where a B&ER locomotive took the train on to Exeter. Both local companies were amalgamated with the LSWR on 1 January 1865 and the broad gauge service from Crediton to Bideford was finally withdrawn in April 1876. This line exemplified the poor rail links that north Devon endured – both at Barnstaple and Bideford the line was on the wrong side of an estuary. Despite this, through coaches ran to and from Waterloo and the 11.00 a.m. departure from Waterloo even contained a luncheon car for Torrington. The line also carried considerable amounts of freight as clay was exported from north Devon via Fremington Quay and coal imported the same way. When the Western region of British Railways took over responsibility for the Southern lines west of Salisbury, the coal traffic was diverted through the Severn Tunnel. The line briefly reopened in January 1968 to alleviate disruption caused by flood damage to Bideford bridge.

Instow Station.

Bideford Station. Refreshments seem to have been well provided for here.

Torrington Station. This picture was taken before the North Devon & Cornwall Junction Railway connected in the immediate foreground.

Bideford, Westward Ho! & Appledore Railway

Passenger service withdrawn	28 March 1917		*Stations closed*	*Date*
Distance	7 miles		Abbotsham Road	28 March 1917
Company	Bideford, Westward Ho! & Appledore Railway		Cornborough	28 March 1917
			Westward Ho!	28 March 1917
Stations closed	*Date*		Beach Road	28 March 1917
Bideford Quay	28 March 1917		Northam	28 March 1917
Strand Road	28 March 1917		Richmond Lane	28 March 1917
Causeway	28 March 1917		Lovers Lane	28 March 1917
Kenwith Castle	28 March 1917		Appledore	28 March 1917

Westward Ho! Station. On the left is the signalbox with the station building to its right. There was only a passing loop here.

An end balcony coach at Appledore Station. Note the flat bottom rails, typical of light railway construction.

This line opened in two stages: the first, to Northam, in May 1901, and the second, to Appledore, in May 1908. During the summer months as many as 16 up and 18 down trains were provided. The line was unusually short-lived and closed so that its equipment could be requisitioned for the war effort. Its Bideford station was, unlike the LSWR station, on the right side of the River Torridge but sadly, although it was standard gauge, the line did not make a connection with it. The only time the line's 2-4-2Ts crossed to the other side of the river was when the line closed in 1917 and temporary tracks were laid so that they could reach the LSWR line prior to being sent overseas. Uncertainty surrounds the fate of two of the line's three locomotives – while one is recorded as being finally scrapped in 1937, the other two are rumoured to have been lost at sea en route to France, possibly due to the action of a U-boat.

One of the line's Hunslet 2-4-2Ts, 'Torridge', with the train's crew beside it at Appledore Station.

North Devon & Cornwall Junction Light Railway

Passenger service withdrawn	1 March 1965	*Stations closed*	*Date*
Distance	20.5 miles	Torrington	1 March 1965
Company	North Devon &	Dunsbear	1 March 1965
	Cornwall Junction Light Railway	Petrockstow	1 March 1965
		Hatherleigh	1 March 1965
		Hole	1 March 1965

The signal box at Torrington Station.

The decaying stations of Dunsbear, below, and Hatherleigh, both photographed in September 1967.

This line ran from Torrington to Halwill Junction and its first 6 miles were built on the route of the 3 feet gauge Torrington & Marland Railway (opened in January 1881) which served the North Devon Clay Company's Marland works. Although it did not convey the general public the Torrington & Marland Railway is of interest in its own right, with its timber viaducts and connections with the engineer J.B. Fell who was known for his Fell centre rail system, monorail experiments, and his long wheelbase locomotives which were designed to reduce the load on the track. Instead it carried workmen for which it used some vans and two redundant London horse trams, their gauge having been reduced. Built under a Light Railway Order of August 1914, the ND&CJLR opened on 27 July 1925 and was promoted by H.F. Stephens who was well-known for his light railway empire that he managed from Tonbridge. It was the last line of any length to be built in the south-west and when it opened no less then four lines radiated from Halwill, to Torrington, Bude, North Cornwall and Okehampton. Now there is no railway there at all. The LSWR had agreed to work the line when it opened but by the time it actually did so the LSWR had become part of the Southern group. For much of its life the line was worked by E1R 0-6-2Ts, rebuilds of Stroudley tanks of the London, Brighton & South Coast Railway. The main town on the line was Hatherleigh, but the station was two miles from it. Passenger traffic was always light, but there was a reasonable amount of cattle traffic for many years.

Bude branch *

Passenger service withdrawn	1 October 1966	*Stations closed*		*Date*
Distance	18.5 miles	Whitstone & Bridgerule		1 October 1966
Company	Devon & Cornwall Railway	Holsworthy		1 October 1966
		Dunsland Cross		1 October 1966
* The closed station that was on this line in Cornwall was the terminus, Bude.		Ashbury		1 October 1966

Whitstone & Bridgerule Station.

The Devon & Cornwall Railway commenced its branch to Holsworthy from Meldon Junction in 1875 and it opened on 20 January 1879. When the line was opened Beaworthy was an intermediate station (it later became Halwill and Beaworthy, then Halwill Junction, and later still Halwill (for Beaworthy)). The extension to Bude was opened by the LSWR on 10 August 1898. Only the last 4.5 miles of the branch was in Cornwall. When the North Cornwall line opened, the line to Bude was worked as a branch. On summer Saturdays in Southern days Bude had its own portion of the Atlantic Coast Express originating at Waterloo, but by the 1960s a DMU sufficed.

North Cornwall line *

Passenger service withdrawn	3 October 1966	*Stations closed*	*Date*
Distance	48.6 miles	Halwill **	3 October 1966
Company	North Cornwall Railway	Ashwater	3 October 1966
		Tower Hill	3 October 1966

Halwill Station, looking towards Okehampton. The white staining of the cattle van on the right was a result of cleaning with lime.

* Closed stations on this line that were in Cornwall were Launceston, Egloskerry, Tresmeer, Otterham, Camelford, Delabole, Port Isaac Road, St Kew Highway, Wadebridge, and Padstow.

** This station was named Halwill Junction until 1923.

On 3 February 1905 a down freight from Ashbury parted at the couplings on the approach to Halwill Junction. The rear portion then caught up and crashed into the front part. There is no record that anyone was hurt, although some pigs were rendered homeless when their sty was knocked down!

The North Cornwall line commenced at Halwill Junction in Devon and headed south to Launceston in Cornwall before passing north of Bodmin Moor to Wadebridge and the LSWR outlier, the Bodmin & Wadebridge Railway, to terminate at Padstow. The North Cornwall Railway was promoted as a separate company (it remained a separate entity until 1922) that the LSWR was to work and the appropriate Act was passed in 1882. The construction was so drawn out that several additional acts were needed. Although the first section from Halwill to Launceston was opened on 20 July 1886, Padstow was not reached until 1899. The line was a boost to the tourist trade of north Cornwall and its famous train, the Atlantic Coast Express, which on summer Saturdays ran in many sections to resorts in north Devon and Cornwall, commenced in 1926. The 'Woolworth' 2-6-0s arrived on the line in 1924 and were to be regular performers almost until the line's closure. Bulleid Light Pacifics arrived in 1945, many of which were named after towns in the area.

Goods being transferred from rail to road transport, in this case horse-drawn, at Ashwater Station.

ASHWATER STATION

LSWR to Plymouth

Passenger service withdrawn	6 May 1968	*Stations closed*	*Date*
	(Bere Alston to Okehampton)	Lydford	6 May 1968
	5 June 1972	Bridestowe	6 May 1968
	(Okehampton to Coleford Junction)	Okehampton	5 June 1972
Distance	35.5 miles	Sampford Courtenay	5 June 1972
Company	London & South Western Railway	North Tawton	5 June 1972
		Bow	5 June 1972
Stations closed	*Date*		
Tavistock *	6 May 1968		
Brentor	6 May 1968	* Renamed as Tavistock North in 1949.	

A class N 2-6-0, no. 31835, at Tavistock North with the Plymouth portion of the Atlantic Coast Express from Waterloo, August 1960.

A West Country class 4-6-2, no. 34015, 'Exmouth', at Okehampton with the 4.20 p.m. service from Plymouth to Waterloo, August 1960.

The history of the LSWR line to Plymouth is deeply mired in the 'Battle of the Gauges', a story littered with broken agreements, shareholdings bought secretly, and lines built but not opened. The line west of Coleford Junction was built by two companies. The first part, from Coleford Junction, about a mile north of Yeoford, was built under the auspices of the Okehampton Railway. It changed its name to the Devon & Cornwall Railway before extending to Lydford (by which time it had been absorbed by the LSWR) where it joined the broad gauge Launceston & South Devon Railway; by use of a third rail, LSWR trains reached Plymouth on 18 May 1876. The LSWR did not get its own route into Plymouth until 2 June 1890, when the second part, built by the Plymouth, Devonport & South Western Junction Railway, was opened from Lydford to Devonport.